The Memory Tray

With the memory of my grandmother,
Elizabeth Douglas Thomas (1907-1984)
and my friend, Jenny Lowe (1968-1988).

Never wait for yourself.
André Breton

The Memory Tray
Deryn Rees-Jones

seren

seren
is the book imprint of
Poetry Wales Press Ltd
First Floor, 2 Wyndham Street
Bridgend, Wales

© Deryn Rees-Jones, 1994
Reprinted 1997

Cataloguing In Publication Data for this title
is available from the British Library

ISBN 1-85411-116-7

*The publisher works with the financial support of the
Arts Council of Wales*

Cover: Detail from Remedios Varo's 'Woman Leaving
the Psychoanalyst', 1961
(Oil on canvas, 17 x 16 in. Private collection.)
With thanks to Walter Gruen of Mexico City

Printed in Palatino by
The Cromwell Press, Melksham

Contents

I

Iconographies

It would be truly marvellous if I were thus able to create illnesses
at the pleasure of my whim and caprice. But as for the truth, I
am absolutely only the photographer; I register what I see.

J-M Charcot

Empty as a seashell, I give myself to you entirely,
lost in the curve of my own fantastic echo. I am
as far away from myself
as ever I thought I could possibly be
and live stretched out on a pale horizon
where a gap grows like a thin blue line
between the blue sky and the too blue sea...

I am X. The unknown quantity. I am Augustine.
I am Louise. At night I dream of rape and fire. I will
tell you my age quietly. Fifteen. Take me
I'm yours. This is my supplication amoureuse:
my hair's tossed back and my hands are raised.
I am beautiful; irresistible as a prayer. Later
I will perform, suck charcoal

like a chocolate bar. On all fours
I will shove up my skirts for you,
bark like a dog; your soft kid glove
becomes a snake in the time it takes
for you to simply say the word and throw it
to the floor. I'm not afraid. I scream. I carry
your top hat, kissing the line of its wet black silks

as if it were a child (my child, your child,
perhaps it is our child
that I hold between us. A bond
of the mind.) You touch me often, maître,
and it hurts. La Salpêtrière. My eyes roll
and my body shudders. I am a pigeon
or an eagle or a dove; for one glorious moment

9

I am learning to fly. You love me, you love me
not. I am your Tuesday star. Sarah Bernhardt
's my heroine. I've never seen her but I hear
her face is perfect and her voice is pure. And me?

I am a walking miracle. With a flash
you take my photograph. By now
I only see the world in black and white.

I smile. Life is an art.
Like everything else, I do it

The Memory Tray

The language game "I am afraid" already contains the object.
                                                            Wittgenstein

There was a milk tooth, with the string that pulled it.
There was a letter in your father's hand.
Welcome to the real world.
There was a chocolate heart wrapped in red tin foil.
There was, *embarrassment,*
A contraceptive. A sanitary towel.
There was a can of laughter.
Can you remember?

Remember I remember I remember.
There was a photograph of somebody I never knew
But knew the name of; there was a tiny paper box,
So beautiful. There was an object
That I can't quite place.
Here instead is my dream.
I remember it in order: (1) *A big man*
(2) *with his big hands* (3) *in a maze who*
Sees (4) *a flock of birds, then,*
Stoops (5) *to tie his shoes, his fingers*
(6's and 7's) *fingering the laces sadly*
Like the drooping heads of flowers...

The Great Mutando

Pulls rabbits out of hats
Ties up the day with handkerchiefs in silk.

So many colours make me cry.
LADIES AND GENTLEMEN, FOR MY NEXT TRICK!

He spins the earth.
Blues. Greens. A plate

On a stick.
Punch. Judy.

Five silver glistening rings.
That link

Then come apart.
Six doves.

Five fly, one suffocates.
A little drop of shit runs down his sleeve.

He makes a Dachshund from three pink balloons.
Mutando!

I want a name like that.
And a world.

Wands. Fairy Godmothers.
No crocodiles.

A place where I can get the handkerchiefs to knot.

The Chair

It might be any Winter, any furnished room —
a table with a tablecloth, a pot-plant in a pot,
my mother's grandmother in charcoal skirts

heating up irons beside the fire, proving
a batch of heavy-headed bread, then
stooping to sit down beside the hearth

absorbed into this scene — the ordinariness
of relief that blends into this strong
domestic — the straight-backed kitchen chair.

Those were the childish Winters that I heard about
but never saw — the way she pulled my mother
on her lap to play a guessing game

of scissor, paper, stone — testing
with hands the fleshly certainty of what things
almost are. No photograph could catch it.

Standing alone today the reconstructed room
now smells of lilac, not the yeasty dough
and hints at loss, the sunlight tightening

like a high bright wound
against the icy and unloving air —
the half-held portions of the past condensed

into an open window, and an empty chair.

Half-term

She speaks to me in a language that is no language.
But I understand it... Speaking her old, old language
of words that are not words.

Jean Rhys

November — a week in Aberystwyth with an aunt
and words I couldn't understand — iawn iawn iawn

bechod iawn — until shooed upstairs
to the saying of prayers and a great brass bed.

Much later, to the click of a clock
and the soft night noise of street and sea,

my dreams came sleepily
like sloppy slippered feet as Nesta

in a long white dress moved spookily,
hiding her nakedness, the terrible lopsidedness

of only one breast. She clambered in
beside me — flat chested in my boneful body

linen cocooned, almost awake, I
rested my head. That gap was delicate

as Summer flowers, and pressed like sealing wax
on letters from the past. And I remember that

she sang to me — oh dee oh doh — as out
over a ridge of anonymous roofs. Winter

serrated an emptiness of sky
to a shiver of cold stars. Snow.

Loving the Greeks

Vos exemplaria Graeca
Nocturna versate manu, versate diurna
Horace

Being girls, we thought it best to love the Greeks
sedately taught us in an attic schoolroom, the Latin master

with his legendary grin making us mistresses
of *the other language* as we heaved an aspirate

apostrophe right from our breathy souls
into the script of the LEXICON GRAECUM. The conjugation

of irregular verbs, the declension of an abstruse noun
came easily. Together we razed citadels, flamed triremes,

routed the barbarians bare-breasted, hand-in-hand,
lifting to glory the cunning of the Greeks. We were always

fast to learn, scorning the rhetoric of Cicero
for the travels of Herodotus; and being *outré*

Ovid's Book of Love, which was, by then,
allowed us, was considered "out" in favour

of the Sapphic fragments, an algebra of meaning
that relieved a frown of footnotes

with the touches of her seventh-century
(B.C.) inflammatory kiss. In mathematics

we also soared, almost in tears
at the arbitrary beauty of a chalked-up phrase

where meaning was a problem of another sort
Let $\theta = \Pi \, \mu^2$!

How often I think of us together, now, being girls,
declining love, writing our lives in pictures

arm-in-arm with an old world
where it was more difficult

to find the perfect answer
to the he loves / she loves part of it.

Largo

Each week, our great Aunt Doris came to teach me piano,
rattling her strings of purple plastic beads, and smelling of carbolic,

her emerald boa draped around her like a mutilated treble clef,
her loose false teeth clacking like a metronome

as she pointed with a knitting needle to the notes of Dvořák's *Largo*
with which I soon grew bored, and played too quickly, and too loud.

Sometimes she'd tell me stories as I played
about the man she loved before the war, the telegram

they sent to let her know that he was killed
in action at the front. And by the end of half-an-hour

I was so proud — my fingers aching from such speed
and was left breathless. Both our eyes were full.

I never really learnt to play the piano, but for that
one inimitable tune, and not long after

great Aunt Doris died, from a tumour leaving her first
stone deaf, then blind. Years later, now, on empty afternoons

I play the *Largo* sometimes, the way that she had wanted it,
smoothly, and slowly, as if somehow those belated sounds

could compensate for all the sad percussions of her life,
the palpitating gaps, the ill-struck chords.

Letters Home

Living between dressing table, counterpane,
only her eyes escape, are empty

station waiting rooms
where wind blows achingly

its ghostly trains at three. "No letters
this time, Lil" (or yesterday, or yesterday:

the nurse) as she re-reads his words — "Dearest"
in air-force blue; "I should be posted home

quite soon, arrive within the week; and though
things turned out badly here my dreams

are still of you." And signed "Undying love."
Undying love. She will forego, thank you,

the lunchtime onions, suck parma violets
instead, will comb her blizzard hair, pacing

that station platform ostentatiously
alone. Short of breath, perhaps — still waiting —

she is half-hesitant and smiles,
sweetens her pulse with eau-de cologne.

Grandma in the Garden

Fence — a thousand little crucifixions,
Stays to the garden:
It's holding its breath

As weeds, the arrogant subversives, contemplate
Their birth. The grass

Is slightly anxious, its green
Unshaven head tremulous

With indecision, beckoning the poplars
To formal disarray, but

They won't come any closer, of that
We can be sure.

The pond smiles, a green ironic
Smear — gruesome as

Overcooked vegetables, pushed
To the side: ridiculous.

O fishes fishes fishes?
They have not swum for twenty years

And their corpses are not welcome here.
We must avert our eyes

To the wild dwarf roses in the rockery
Which sit, autistic, unafraid.

Draped elegantly in fuchsia and in black
Here Grandma watches from a chair,

One wild Modigliani eye hooking
The clouds, and lost

In the terrible gap between grass
And sky that the children know,
That they put in their pictures.

Making for Planet Alice

You stand on a chair with a wrinkled nose
In your glittery tiara. Queen Alice and her Queendom!

The room is full of ordinariness
And your laughter like a tossed coin

Spins into the air. Take me to that place, I say,
Where the trees grow upside-down and their thick bright roots

Explore the sky. Take me to that place
Over the backs of houses, past the forgotten railway,

Across the continents by rickshaw
Where the sun sets in a moment, then slowly rises

Like a blush. Where the door in the wall opens to yards
Of purple strawberries, a yellow field of grasshoppers —

Their low sweet hum. Where the green pool of your imagination
Laps the edges of your head like sleep, its yawning mountains

Rock like lullabies and clocks, and pampas grasses
Stroke your forehead in the winds. Quietly, quietly

Take me to that strange safe place, by bus, by unicycle
Helicopter, aeroplane. Let me sail to Planet Alice in my heart,

My leaky coracle; let me circumnavigate the moon,
The foam of snow white stars. Take me to that strange place

That hurts me. That we both knew once upon a time.
Which I've not only lost, but forgotten how to say.

Summer

Is a lazy god, and all promises.
He says he will never leave,
Was a long time coming
With swallows in his air —
Petulant, weeping.

Waking early one morning
I watch him from the bedroom window
Barefoot on the wet grass,
Stalking the garden and beside himself
With all the brilliant flowers.

With soft, dry hands he soothes their heavy heads.
My children's books, too,
That were carelessly left on the lawn all night,

Unread and ruined by the rain.

II

First

Like the impossible floodings of a fleet of clouds'
regurgitative rain, I can remember
all there was to know about that morning —
how the first light cracked across the flung-back
shutters of our window, remaking all the shadows
of our crumpled skin-white bed. Sex

had nothing to do with it —
only the way I took your body as my body
in my hands — not knowing what to do with it,
myself, as each shy stroke began to form a canvas
stretching its colours to the livid natures of the night.
At least that was the way I wanted to remember it
and called it being in love. And would I be lying
if I added too, just how intrigued I was,
quietly concerned? Like the first time
as a child, cutting my finger, smelling the blood.

Jim

The way she loved him was the colour green —
Not some blue china Wednesday in the sky;
Her body took him for the mountains, lay in him
To suckle him with flowers. Perhaps she loved him
Like tomorrow, though her head was lacking
In particulars — such things as names and dates
Eluded her, he knew. But looking for the snow

The weatherman had promised her, it was something
The rain implied, migrating to her eyes as she grew wary
Even of the female authors on his bookshelves
Lining the orange of his bedroom wall
With hardbacks, broken paper spines.
Walking alone one afternoon in early Spring
A passing friend asked where she lived. She smiled,

The clouds reflected in her eyes: her mouth
Was thinking of the taste of hills, and
Efo cariad, she said, remembering the sound
His brink-of-love would make, allowing
Her forgetfulness this time, the pattern
Of his single syllable, abbreviated name.

Holiday

Carrots were cheap that Winter — 9p for a pound, perfect
ingredients for soups. You chopped them finely
with a deft brown hand, cream parsnips too, and yellow onions,
lobbing them gently in an old black pan
with sprinklings of black pepper,
mountain herbs, and sunflower seeds, all hissing
on the gassy stove. And you precise and serious and tender.
How I loved to watch you cooking in that faded navy sweater,
your studied domesticity, and what's that phrase
my mother always used to use —
It warmed the cockles of my heart!

Wrapped up, we walked the white sand coast
and holidayed our faces in the wind, looking away
from all the structures of the land
to the soothing sibilants, the infinities
of water. Returning to the study and our skin
began to burn — *ssh*, the fire said to the worn-out
velvet of the high-winged chairs, the stacks
of half-read open books. Our kisses were insistency in that
much more familiar upstairs narrow bed. We teased —
pushing our closenesses away, bringing them close —

our curve and straight a perfect fit — a sort of sadness
and a strange delight. Outside the oceans shrugged,
rubbing their shoulders with no boundaries, the ravelling
and unravelling of each other in entirety, letting
each other go. I ask if love is anything but this, but
midnight, and my words slip into dreams, and swim away —
the coyness of a shoal of deep-sea fish, as my hands
work over their beautiful names —
Atlantic, Pacific and Indian blue, easing them
like grave Italians their bright enamel rosaries
in waterfalls through hands. Elsewhere

the deep and plunge of night. The distances
are hollow and it makes me quiet
when waking up, so terribly alone. It is
a sort of reassurance when you lean back into me
and whisper with authority, that looking down
from space the earth does not rotate, but seems to float
familiar as a blown up beach-ball —
light in the dark, the perfect ocean blue.

Following

Your silence rebukes me like a seraph's smile.
All Winter I have dreamed of you and her —
The fleshy double bed — wanting

To prise her from you with my tongue, to lick
The years' interiors, smooth
As the hennaed intimacy

Of a peach stone to a peach; to
Smash them irretrievably —
Those unimaginable symmetries —

The lost curve of a perfect shell
That no one ever managed to depict.
I say these words over to myself

Like spells, wanting to know the meaning
Of them wholly and exactly: husband and wife —
Changing their emphasis, pronunciation,

Their relation each to each. Outside it snows:
The shattering first fall, and our walls bloom
Like crocuses unfurling in the dark. *Her name was*

Helen. It could only last ten years. That was
Your sad, half-hearted joke. Now
There is nothing to be said. In the half-light
Your daughter reads, looks up from time to time.

She has her mother's soft uncanny ways.
And her blue eyes that mesmerize me.
I watch them as they hatch like silk.

Untitled

Winter. The weather spat.
You copied out your dreams into a fat black book
And spoke to no one. Bleak as an X-ray,
The stars poked through the night like bones.

Each morning from the bedroom window
You voyaged to the edge of the world,
Your eyes straining for a glimpse of the sea —
Laid out in the distance, a flat blue line.

I wanted to put my thumbprint on it
Like a child, unable to write,
Longing to grubby the untouched page.

Interim

For a week now my heart has arrived too late
For your love. We have been missed departures,
Cancelled trains. Luggage in Paris, me in Singapore.
Old jokes. And suddenly every word
And metaphor is unimportant or confused or wrong.
Darling our bodies say in the dark, making up
In spite of ourselves, in sleep.
Darling belly Darling breasts Darling thighs.
Darling. Darling. Darling. What does this mean?
Find me a way to remake the words;
To change with clean sweet sheets
The turbulent, the tired, the slept-in bed
Of Love, the Golden Barge.

A siren flashes blue and mute
Like the moon on a bender,
Staggering drunkenly around the room
As still our bodies sympathise.
I love you. I love you. Cliché. *I*
Love you. Live again. I will stroke you, tending
Your body like a wound. I love you. Live. Love.
And after the fever of loving, tell me I...

The elephant god
Stares down at us
Eight limbs confusing themselves
And each other in a bed. And I stare back.
Ganesa, Son of Siva.
I see tusk, trunk.
A pair of wise unblinking eyes.

Shadowplay

I come to you like a child, as only an adult could

With the silence
Growing and shrinking
This is it. Infidelity.
These are the strange geographies of hurt.

You hold my head in your hands
As if it were a globe
Rocking me slowly
From side to side. As if love
Were a country, difficult to place.

Now you smile, and this is enough to make me weep.

On the blank walls of the familiar room
Your soft hands are intimate with shadows. Softly

They surprise me

Making duck with an arch of a wrist
Making wolf with a clasp of the hands. Fingers
Are beak, then snout and brow,
Those two familiar bitten thumbs
Sprout up inquisitive as ears.

This is your way of playing forgiveness.
In these half-light moments
You are rabbit, monster, dove.

Later, I make bets on all the things you'll never recreate —
Cash in on earthquakes, truth.
Lose out on hope, desire

Your porcelain heart with its hair-line fractures.

And Please Do Not Presume

And please do not presume it was the way we planned it,
Nor later say *We might have tried harder*,
Or *Could have done better.*
Nor remind us of the things we didn't take:
The hints, the trains, the tonics,
The tape-recordings of ourselves asleep,
The letters of a previous lover,
The photos of each other as a child.

And please do not presume our various ways of making up,
Of telling lies and truths, the way we touched
Or laughed, the Great Mistakes, the Tiger Suit,
Our list of *Twenty Favourite Movie Classics*,
Breakfast in bed, red wine, the different ways we tried
To make each other come
Were anything else than the love we wanted;

Or that we did no more or less than anybody might have done.

And more, do not presume we could have stopped it —
Like a clock, a gap, a leak, or rot; or made it
Last much longer than it did;
Or that the note on the fridge that one of us left,
Wasn't sweetly meant, but badly spelt:
Step One of *Ten Proggressive Ways to Disolution.*

Armistice

Sweetheart, don't mind me if I think tonight
That the pale line of your silken shoulders
Turning away
Has never been more eloquent.

If this bed is our human nest,
Then you are folded like a wing,
With only the soft hairs of your skin
Feathering out
Like a whisper of friendship. The rest of you's

So still. You
Who taught me at seventeen
To make myself a body map.
How to stand in the cinnamon fields, aching in moonlight.
How to bathe in the waterfall, laughing at the sun.

How much I want to touch you, now!
And how you would crow, if only you knew!

Without you it's so very cold.

Let us throw up our hands, impatient with war.
Let our kisses feed us like bread and honey.

Darling, come into the open, show yourself!
Beautiful and indignant
Your soft hooves smelling of love
Hurry down, like a gazelle or a wild goat,
Hurry down from the spice-bearing mountains!

Afterward

Here, in the darkness,
I might be with you for the first time.
I feel your full lips blossoming,
Your cool hands entering.
As we fall into the night,
We clutch each other, mystified.
Words without words
It is like hanging off the edges of the stars,
Our cries unanswerably sweet.

Later, in a moment of moonlight,
We are ordinary again,
Striped by the shadows of the blue venetian blind.
Our tongues are the rough tongues of tigers.
Our gleaming eyes are beacons, dangerous,
Our purring skins like milk.

Custody

As if we could not possibly have known
Your daughter sermonizes, telling us
How years ago the Thames froze over,
How you could skate, stamp, dance, keep pigs, light fires
Do anything. Like a palm to be read
The river's currents mummified
To loops and bumps and whorls.
It was so very cold.

Another time, you might have launched into your old routine
Making the pair of you a comic double act
The patter of an early Technicolor film;
Ginger and Fred, dancing your way
Through dialogue — and her let down
By the phrase you always end with — *coup de grâce* —
Concerning *grandmothers* and *sucking eggs...*
Each time the phrase like magic.
Each time provoking teenage tantrum, kisses, making-up.

But this time I watch as you smile
In a fractured provocative
Fatherly way; ruffle her tangled yellow hair
As if she were some Genii's lamp
Able to give you wishes,
Saying *I'll miss you.* And we all agree

Winter is on us: the rain, the broken leaves,
The figure-hugging nights surrendering
To frosts, sub-zero window tinsels,
Whole grieving swaying crops of prickle-fingered trees.
It's never been harder to say goodbye.

Later, uneasy in the rented bed, the rented house
We can't quite make our own
You wake startled
From your dreams; your cold white face
A thawing waterfall. I want to comfort you,
Pulling you back to sleep
And soothing *She'll be back.*

You reassure me in my turn,
Say you're afraid of nothing and of nobody,
Now that she's gone.
Nobody's step, our resident ghost,
The creak on the empty midnight stairs.

The Dinosaur Summer

That year the film-makers built dinosaurs,
With crops of tripods and gesticulations,
The double-stranded kick-starts mapped
Onto a blue print of the Mesozoic, reconstructed
Pea-brained, and extravagant. *Apatosaurus ajax*
Tricerotops horridus. Appropriately Hollywood. After
Prolonged castings it was rumoured that the leading man

Went down with Mumps. The leading lady quietly
                                 disappeared.
And all the while ferocious debutantes, the dinosaurs
Emerged victoriously from behind the screen
Of trees and backdrop trees. Grumbling from shot to shot
                            each take
Became as painful as the pulling of a Hairy Mammoth's tooth.
Nobody laughed. The dinosaurs were unresponsive, and
                              chewed on
Papaya, fake arrowroot. Occasionally they snarled, best-side

To camera, all their computerised mechanics squeezed
To anarchy and camouflaged in beautifully dyed skins.
Even the famous palaeontologists were heard to say they'd
Had it with their ancient temperaments
Like babies. Squalling. The insufferable heat, they said
Was quite insufferable without their colleagues' wives.
For six long weeks we squabbled in the air-conditioned hum;

Iced coffee Spanish style. Ate, drank, breathed, lived
The Prehistoric. Then hardly said a word for weeks. At last
Could only lie, deep-breathing anxiously and side-by-side. We
Barely touched at all except, I'm told,
In someone else's dreams. Impossibility
Dawned with the morning, sank with the purpling
                                evening skies...
One time at dusk, after a shoot

Cancelled due to seventeen freak minutes of white rain,
I found a footprint in the damp bright earth
So large and real I thought that no one had invented it,
And stretched inside it like a grave. When the rainy
                                        season came
For Real the whole crew left. The director
Was a broken man, was last heard jabbering a feeble *Cut!*
                                        ·in tears.
I remember how we laughed together, then,

Rolled on the floor in stitches, clutched at our sides.
Each mad hypothesis about the dinosaurs' extinction
Rang strangely true under their watchful eyes.
I remember how we saw the experts off, their silver trucks
Grumbling into the middle distance as they waved,
Whispering frantically between themselves that the beginning
Of the dinosaurs was the beginning of the birds. How,

In the downpour, the curious pink jungle flowers —
                                        the only foliage
The dinosaurs despised — began to bloom exquisitely,
Birthing the smell of paradise. I remember
We surprised ourselves. Each other. Were suddenly aroused.

III

William and Georgie, 1917

The automatic writing gave shape to thoughts which were to find their public expression in *A Vision*. The thoughts and imagery of *A Vision* underpin much of the poetry Yeats wrote after his marriage, giving it an air of assurance.... Yeats's marriage was itself consolidated not only in the common interest, the shared work and the sense of discovery that the automatic writing and its interpretation involved, but also by the content of the script which related to his often obsessional assessment of his relationships with Maud, Olivia Shakespear, Mabel Dickinson, Iseult and his wife.... All this involved a great deal of work, and the sheer volume of scripts Mrs Yeats preserved made an impressive sight.

A. Norman Jeffares, *W.B. Yeats: A New Biography*

She is wearing a coat of rainbow camel-hair
and a rose-quartz crystal
on a bootlace round her neck. The chambermaid
thinks *How lovely she is,*
admiring her hair, and the cut
of her dress. Then wrinkles up her nose

and scurries off. *Georgina.*
This man beside her
in the pince-nez
is her husband. He etches their name
into the guest book
in perfect copperplate while pulling off his cape.
Each flourish is controlled. *William
and Georgie...*

His mind's on other things. Poetry for one.
Iseult. The nature and the quantity of love.
A strange thing surely. There's nothing
she can do. Instead —
nothing to lose —
she says
that she will write for him...

His eyes like the turning tide.
A prophecy!

***

Her hand moves in silence
gliding like the coloured sands
of the egg-timer her friend
brought back for her after a summer's day
on England's south-west coast. She kept it
in her pocket for a year
until it cracked and burst. From one part

to another
her memories move, particle by particle
to things she knows
she must not think about right now.

If only she could concentrate!
The colours in the sand!

(She remembers the walk they took beside the ocean,
remembers how she wore her new galoshes
to disguise her ballerina feet. Country of rains,
betrayals, towers. The green
bread of her childhood. The smell of peat
and milky puddings...

***

She is worrying about her babies
how they will grow
inside her so that she learns
to wear her body like an out-grown dress,

wondering whether
when they're old enough they'll have to fight
somebody else's war. *How much
will it hurt?)*

A small voice echoes
in her head, telling her
it will always be this way.
Anxieties! she wishes
she could banish them, let them
float out of her head for just one hour

She remembers
She remembers
She remembers

Like an itch, slowly and deliberately
She scratches the page with her pen
We have come to give you metaphors for poetry.

***

Tomorrow he will write
to friends, telling
the easiness of marriage,
And when she wakes up from her dreams
she finds him
sleeping peacefully beside her.
Her hands cup
the cool dark sack between his legs.
A comforter. How she loves him!
The white sheets gleam in the moonlight
as she strokes his cheek,
brushing away the
sprigs of sea-lavender
which sprout from his ears, from the tips
of his cow's-lick hair.

I Know Exactly the Sort of Woman
I'd Like to Fall In Love With

If I were a man.

And she would not be me, but
Older and graver and sadder.
And her eyes would be kinder;
And her breasts would be fuller;
The subtle movements
Of her plum-coloured skirts
Would be the spillings of a childhood summer.

She would speak six languages, none of them my own.

And I? I would not be a demanding lover.
My long fingers, with her permission
Would unravel her plaited hair;
And I'd ask her to dance for me, occasionally,
Half-dressed on the moon-pitted stairs.

The Ladies

One hand slammed against the faulty lock
We scan messages on doors, chiselled
In biro and succinct
As gravestone epitaphs — that *men are bastards*
And that *Sue loves Steve, Marie's a slag*
And *Ann shags anything that moves:* assess

The catalogue of rich obscenities, puzzle
The help lines with their numbers
Scribbled out; retch
At the blue detergent, pig-shit sweet amidst
Incisive twists of toilet paper, the
Niagara flush
Of the unfettered toilet chains. It is

No wonder we avoid each other's eyes
Busy with soap and regurgitative roller towels;
Strange that next
We rearrange ourselves
In mirrors, put lipstick on, and then,

With sidelong glances
Try on each other's smiles.

Connections

Deer walk upon our mountains, and the quail
Whistle about us their spontaneous cries;
Sweet berries ripen in the wilderness.
                                        Wallace Stevens

I've dialled wrong, but she will talk.
My voice is her event, hers mine.
Am I English? *Saesneg*, I explain.

Winter, she says. In the wilderness.
The snow has never been so thick,
Caking her lonely wooden house.
The gutters spill water
The colour of flour. There are
Everywhere fir trees everywhere.
Breath becomes ice. In the woods,
Alone, a gunshot makes you listen.
There is silence.

The comforting roar of the hoarse brown bear.

I have stars, I say, English stars, a Welsh mountain I can
Just remember — *mynydd* — a word I can't pronounce too well.

In this room
I have newspapers
Three days old. A vase of dying flowers. The radio.
I have the voices of the politicians. Books. An atlas
I can't find either of us on.

We see each other for one split second:
How her red lips, laughing, grow redder in the cold.
How my hair has lost its summer lights, and my fingers tap
Needing a cigarette.

We rub noses in the moment of goodbye
Wanting our mouths to speak us closer,
Closer closer closer than the telephone.

Goggle-Head

after the sculptures of Dame Elisabeth Frink, 1930-1993

1.

Riding the Underground like soup loose in a cargo ship, my soul,
(So terribly unfashionable) lurches through London, stop by stop —
Brixton to Seven Sisters: a straight-backed ocean, blue, correct,
Carrying us trembling like the century. With the discomfiture
Of a cat put out, you sit across from me, a Goggle-Head
In shades, (some spectacle!) your features blank because of it.
Show me your eyes, Mystery, as the Gumshoe would say.
Show me your eyes. I know that you can see me:
The borders of my body on the chequered seats.
And all of us encased in steel and glass.

2.

Will I turn to stone, Medusa Man, seeing for the first time
Where it comes from, that light behind the eyes,
The politics, the histories? Will I wear it like a bomb
Shattering the windows from within, exposing you, all heart?
The girl you slept with in the night who put such things there that
You cannot show them; the child you murdered in an alleyway;
The brother kissing you goodbye; or how your mother wept
The time you lied to her you lied you lied...
Such secrets frighten me, such a reserve of truth
Or such interiority. Is it a friendship or a death you offer?
I hold it like a teardrop on a finger, captive for a moment
In the light. Staring staring I will bear it as I must
And its enormity. Your gravity and your stupidity;
Your anonymity; your vulnerability; your love; your restive grace.

Lovesong to Captain James T. Kirk

Captain. I never thought we'd come to this,
but things being what they are, being adults,
stardate '94 it's best to make the best of it
and laugh. What's done is done. Perhaps
I'll start to call you Jim or Jamie, James...

No one was more shocked than me when I arrived
(*the lady doth protest*) to find
my bruised and rainy planet disappeared
and me, materialised and reconstructed
on board the Starship Enterprise, all 60s
with my lacquered bee-hive and my thigh-high
skirt in blue, my Doctor Marten's and my jeans
replaced by skin-tight boots
and scratchy blue-black nylons rippling-
up my less-than-perfect calves. Sulu
looked worried. Spock cocked up one eyebrow
enigmatically, branding my existence
perfectly illogical. How nice, I thought. His ears.
Uhura smiled of course, and fiddled
with her hair. *O James.* Truth is
I loved you even as a child...

O slick-black-panted wanderer holding
your belly in, your phaser gun
on stun, and eyes like Conference pears! You're not my type
but I undress you, and we fuck
and I forgive your pancake make-up and mascara,
the darker shadows painted round your eyes.
The lava-lamp goes up and down. We're
a strange unison. Politically
Mismatched. Our mutual friend
The Doc takes notes. *Go easy Bones!*
Scotty is beaming and shouts *Energise,*
and all of a sudden you remind me

Of my dad, my brother and my mum,
my body rising like a shadow from the past
on top of you. As I press your arms behind your head
I drape my breasts so that you
brush my nipples gently with your lips almost
involuntarily as we boldly go. Come slowly, Captain,
and we do, with both our pairs of eyes tight closed.

Meeting the Queen

No doubt to some I am the perfect debutante
although my ballgown is a little out of date, not quite
the *haute couture*, but individuality's
the thing. I garnish it with beauty
no one else has noticed on the streets,
and as I move it rattles, gleams. If pulchritude
became a smell, I'd reek. One day I
caught a rainbow. Wore it,
my cheeks lit up with rouge. But that's
a long time now. One thing I can't remember. How
to blush, like when I was a girl. But I can dance —
Cha-cha, one-two, one-two, a slinky step. Not disco
Rock 'n' Roll. The men
they clasped you tight those days,
pushing their body into yours: the waltz
just so — my favourite, their thighs
where no one else could see. Your body
sent you messages your mother'd not forgive.
The weight of one gloved hand
in the small part of your back
was an apocalypse. I remember.
I was your baby, everybody's girl...

But now, needs must, I wear a wig. I have my pride,
combing the tat from it in puddles, laying it out carefully
to dry. I watch its breezy ringlets, like a Man o'War
following the Thames downstream. It's cold. I sleep
under the arches in old newspaper. Old hat. Sometimes
the print comes off and writes itself across my skin. Often
my feet turn blue. Mornings, I'm out of tune, not sure
exactly who or where I am. It passes,

and the day goes on. I hunt out ornaments
from bins for friends and look two ways
to cross the road, the way that I was taught. I curtsey
prettily. The tower blocks bow. *Your royal highness*
pleased to meet you, ma'am. Oh, on the contrary, my dear,
we've heard a lot. The pleasure is entirely ours.
Please stay. We'd hate it if you go.

Service Wash

For six months now I've washed her clothes,
The old favourites, the new acquaintances:
One large bag of colours, one small bag of whites.
By now I've got to know the oyster camisole,
The chambray trouser suit, the pink silk blouse
That has its own expensive scent, the purple jogging suit
That smells of sweat and traffic. Her knickers
With the blood left on. Sometimes I think about her
And the way she does her hair, wanting to know
The thousand things about her that I don't already know.
The bell-boy says she's often out, that when he tips his hat
She smiles. My wife would kill me
If she knew the way I thought. *Pervert,*
She'd say. And then the rest. Perhaps she's right.
With the place to myself one afternoon
I tried a dress of hers, all fresh and newly ironed,
And then felt warm and close to her. I could have cried.
My breasts hung empty, huge pink satin flowers...

Mostly I keep myself to myself. Head down
And my back's covered. Christ knows, I need the job.
Sometimes, though, just sometimes, it can get too much
                                    and absent-
Mindedly I mismatch my clients' socks.
That gets them ringing for *Room service!*
Never her. I think she's like that, likes
To wear them odd. Once an old bloke
Sent me down a note which said that socks
Were Lost Platonic souls. I like the way that sounds.
Perhaps one day I'll say the same to her.
I'd love to make her laugh. Sometimes I see her smiling
Through the steam. Then she dissolves. Love's spectre.
There's no end to what you learn down here.

Sometimes I think an afternoon will last for ever.
Sometimes I think the world is flat. Go on. Convince me.
Sometimes I think I'll fall in love again.

Leonardo

My step-mother nursed me,
And kept me for love,
Called me *Inquisitor*,
Laughed as I grew:
Wild Goat of the slopes of Monte Albano!

With my first angel
I dragged passion from the heavens laughing
Ran out through Florence sandal-less
And shouted *Truth!* I blew up the world,
Then created it
Flocked it with cannon,
Foetuses, flying machines;
I dissected thirty corpses,
Formed moments
From stone like water,
Mirrored
All the crooked movements of the soul.

Now I hold life quietly
As the night protects.
The boys play pranks,
Or rough and tumble
So I smile. They read,
Mix paint from tree-bark,
Comb breadcrumbs
From my oozy beard. Sometimes
To tempt me,
Salai brings fresh cherries
Quails' eggs, or raspberries,
Baskets of blue plums. Bright-eyed
And heavy-lidded
The perfection of his body
Furnishes all things. Yet every day

The sunlight hurts me more.
I feel for the harsh lines
Of deliberate sketches
Sending swan-dance movements
Through my absent-mind.

Porphyria

Running in and out of the rain I was breathless,
Laughing. I wanted you. Bit by perfect bit
I wanted you
To devour me. I was an archangel

Slipping beautifully down
From the heavens
Until I was the only woman in the world
Giving you everything

In time. There was nothing wrong
In that. Leaves from the elm trees
Wreathed my satin purple skirts
Stained by the weather

As I sat beside the open fire
Watching you watch me
As I undid my storm damped hair.

And my hands shook
As you held me in your gaze,
Pulling it tight around me.

Now you pay a girl from the villages
To weave my hair into a dress that later
She'll refuse to wear for you. At night

She spins by the window, shivers
When you enter her. Don't think you can forget.
Porphyria. My last breath

Is the yawn of a hurricane; the bruises on my throat
Are ugly flowers that sprout each morning
From your finger tips. You thought you could have me

For ever and ever. Amen. Amen. I'm here.
I feel the whole world whispering
As delicately the light winds bless my shaven skull.

Each morning, your screaming when you wake
Disturbs me. Silent as a prayer, I slip upstairs,
Return to you, bringing a bowl of camomile to soothe.

But my small hands are the hands of a fever.
My nails birth a scar. In God's name, I'm back.
I am the eyes of all the women in the house.

Metamorphoses

In examining the earliest mental shapes assumed by the sexual life of children we have been in the habit of taking as the subject of investigations the male child, the little boy. With little girls, so we have supposed, things must be similar, though in some way or other they must nevertheless be different.

Freud, *Some Psychical Consequences of the Anatomical Differences Between the Sexes*

No one believes I'm Marilyn Monroe, 36-28-36. At fifty,
5' 10, a beard and thirteen stone, not even me. But you have
                                       to dream.
A Girl Can't Help It. I think of her like nothing else:
Her breasts. A strip of thigh. The way a body moves. *Love Goddess.*
Her teeth like buttons on an open shirt. Her prawn-pink lips.
That mole. And her face like a white flower, blossoming,
                                       blossoming.
Her heels tap out my destiny. A sexy, breathy tune. I want
To step out from this body like a snake would lose its skin.

My Shrink wears wigs and slacks. I wear a yellow dress,
                                       have polish
On my fingernails. She speaks in baritone, Butch to my *Femme.*
                                       My legs
Cross at the ankle, hers the knee. More of a man than me.
I wanted a couch I could lie right back on. A vase of lilies,
Or Egyptian artefacts. A way I could explain myself.
My self. My. Self. Instead an upright chair. A large-spooled
                                       tape-machine.
The window ladling the sunlight like syrup from a tin. My eyes
A glass of water, shrinking on the window sill...

She made me watch *The Op.* on video, the curtains drawn. Where
Parts of Me would go. Adjustments. Hormones. Sutures. Scars.
                                       It changes
Nips and Tucks alright. The canopies of flesh. No going back.
                                       Making me
Question everything. I cried. Considering myself in terms of pain.
                                       Just like

Bereavement. Moving house. Divorce. Or finding a new name.
                                        The endless re-
Arrangements. Three years later and I find (excuse the cliché,
                                        please) I'm
Falling in love again. The woman I once married. Her tears
As sticky-sweet as candyfloss. Her ordinary beauty makes me pale.

She says she loves me and she likes it. Hot. The little places
Where I've learned to push my tongue. Her two hands brush
                                        my breasts
Like angel wings, like tiny falling stars. Her mouth. The way
                                        I feel it
Here. The space between us changes shape each night,
Opens and closes — kaleidoscopic loops and whirls. Sometimes
Diamonds Are a Girls Best Friend. You know? *Boop-Boop-Be-Doop.*
Our joke. And *Happy Birthday.* Marilyn. Last night, as perfect
Yet more perfect than a wedding ring — our bodies rising,
Falling. There, growing between us, an exquisitely shaped O.

Soap

The bouncer with the slashed face, they say he killed a man
But still you dance
When he asks you to dance. You remind him

You couldn't knock a hole in Wednesday's wet Echo
That bird on the telly, the tits on her
But always you open the door for a lady

The girl he says he's seeing
She says he makes her safe

We were cut-up, of course, at the news —
The railway track, the noose.

You calling me a scally?

But we live with death and the pros
On Hope Street. Football's the thing.

In Liverpool we have a lorra lorra laughs
I won't be held responsible if he goes free

Now I ask you, princess, chasing dragons.
Do Woolly Backs make better kissers?
Sinbad. Mother. Can a girl love a girl?

Is the Pope a Catholic?

Why is it so hard to feel so close.

The body in the garden gets up and walks.
For a year he washed his hands until they bled.

Blue

For Ian

Noon in Greenwich Park. A freak heat-wave.
We've Take-Out from *Pistachios* and all around
Mothers and children spreading themselves out under
                                        the trees and us,
Out to Lunch. We are
Laughing about Frank O'Hara. Lancashire.
Talking LOVE, SEX, TIME, in the hours before your train.
I watch your straight white teeth, curious, your clean brown
                                        hands.
            It feels like weeks ago.
This morning as I'm showering
The sun strikes me like a belly-dancer
And I smile, moving my hips against the soap.
My hair is only just drying as I buy groceries —
Oranges and Paracetamol — and it is 12:39 or 12:43
Depending on what clock I check
When the car breaks-down in the multi-storey.
When the A.A. man I've waited 50 minutes for says
You've got a silly name I smile
For the second time that day. In dungarees,
With oil on my hands and cheeks,
I'm feeling sexy and amazed. He starts the AX
With jump-leads. *That's quick,* I say and he grins
Writing *3 YEARS GARRANTY* on a green slip
For a new battery: *We don't hang about!*
The car's dead heart on the grimy floor,
Pink like a wound, replaced.
                        Driving home
With the windows down
I think how many names there are —
Inchoate — Bougainvillaea — Love —
For not so many things.
And cooking supper for my lover sing him
Choruses and highlights from the *Fiddler on the Roof.*
A blessing on his head...

Later

I cry for all my indiscretions.
                              Remembering being 19;
Your reading Whitman and Moore
In the seminar room: the *Yah-honk!*
Of the wild goose, quavering. The steeple-jack,
The steeple's *solid-pointed star.* Tonight I'm balancing all this
In my head, watching the sky purple like a bruise
And thinking of you, as I read *Time Out*
On Jarman's latest and most probably his last:
"In the pandemonium of image
I present you with the universal blue..."

The Poet Writes a Letter

Writing about the past brings its own dangerous nostalgias
Was part of a message that you left me
On the ansaphone last night; my letter
Sent to you first class, the previous afternoon,
Had quoted the Greeks and failed to reach you...

I had two things other that I'd meant to say.
And so the poet writes another letter
Which will this time remain unsigned:

Dear X,

I love you.

Do you remember?
I drew a heart on your back in my own blood once
As we bathed.

Acknowledgements

Acknowledgements are due to the editors of the following publications, where some of these poems first appeared: *Bête Noire, The Gregory Anthology 1991-1993, Iron, Jacaranda Review, London Magazine, The Malahat Review, Manchester Poets 3 anthology, New Welsh Review, Poetry Wales, Poetry Review, South-West Poetry Competition 1993 anthology,* and *Verse.*
Thanks also to the Society of Authors for financial assistance.

"Iconographies" draws on material from Elaine Showalter's chapter "Feminism and Hysteria: The Daughter's Disease" in *The Female Malady: Women, Madness and Culture, 1830-1980* (Virago, 1987).
"Chair" was, and so is, for Selima Hill.
"Armistice" steals from the Song of Solomon.
"Blue" is also for the memory of the late Derek Jarman.

Many thanks to Rachel Grimshaw and to Ian Gregson; to Dawn McHale and Pete Rodgers who did more than they probably realise; but especially to James Kimmis for his unfailing enthusiasm, honesty, inspiration and support. This book is also for him.